Sonatinas

Sonatines
Sonatinen

I

K 131

INDEX

Anton Diabelli (1781–1858): 4 Sonatines, Op. 151
Le Bouquetier – The Flowerpot – Der Blumenkasten

Anton Diabelli (1781–1858): 7 Sonatinen, Op. 168
Musikalische Morgenstunden einer Woche – Musical small hours of a week –
Matinées musicaux d'une semaine

6 Progressive Sonatinas*
Op. 36

Muzio Clementi
(1752–1832)

*The present edition of M. Clementi's six sonatinas is based on the fifth edition Sublished in the composer's life-time
(London, Clementi Co., c1813). On the title-page the following can be read: "with considerable improvement by the author"
It is due to this fact that the music text of the present edition deviates from the commonly used versions in a lot of places.

Andante

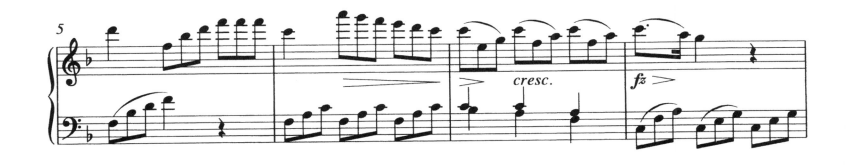

Allegretto

2.

mezzo

cresc.

f

mezzo

fz — *p*

Allegretto con grazia

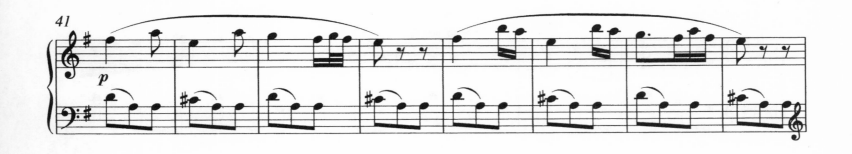

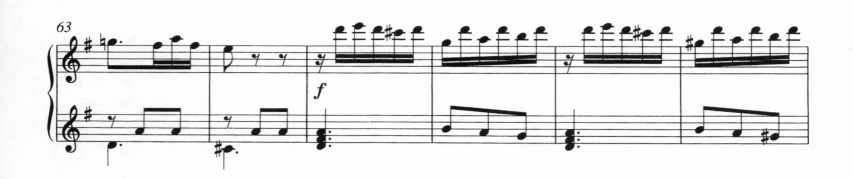

Allegro spiritoso

3.

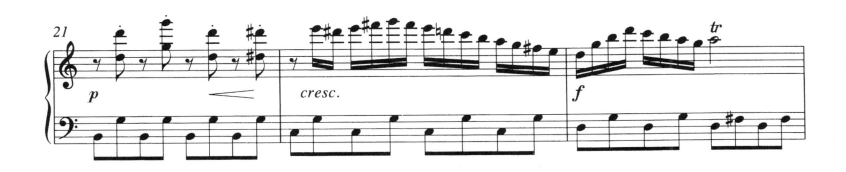

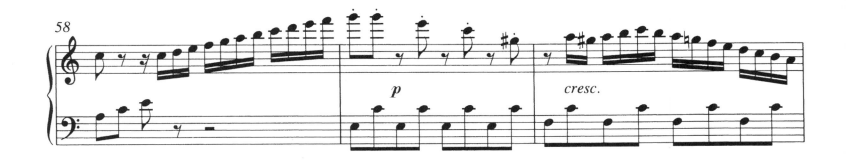

Andante

Allegro di molto

mezzo

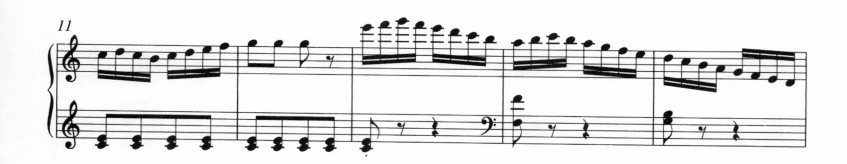

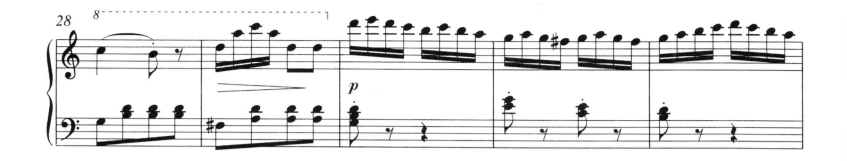

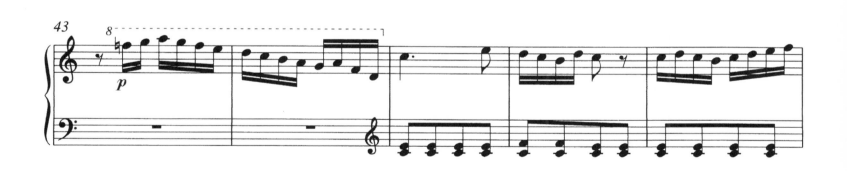

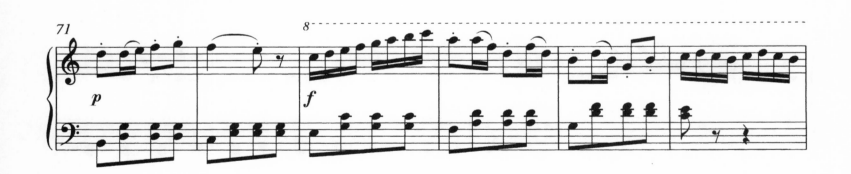

Con spirito

4.

Andante con espressione

Da Capo al Fine

5.

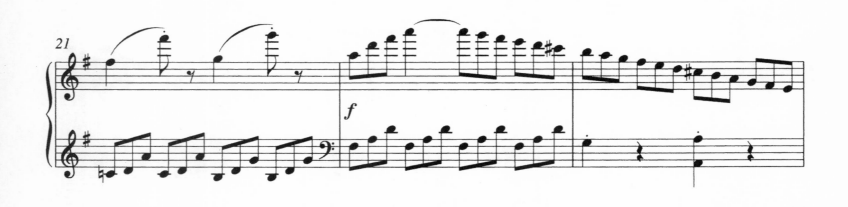

Swiss air arranged

Allegretto moderato

Rondo

Allegro assai

Fine

Da Capo al Fine

Allegro con spirito

6.

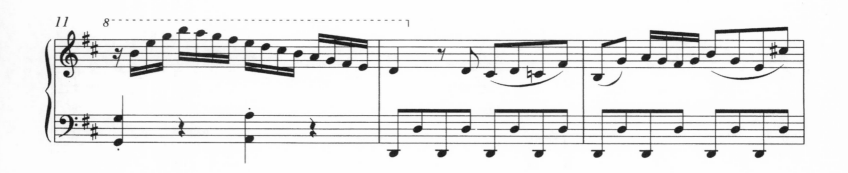

Rondo

Allegretto pastorale

6 Sonatinen

Op. 55

Friedrich Kuhlau
(1786–1832)

Vivace

Allegretto

2.

Cantabile

legato assai

dim.

Allegro scherzando

Allegro con spirito

3.

Allegro grazioso

Allegro non tanto

4.

dolce e legato   *cresc.*

Andantino con espressione

Alla pollacca

Da Capo al Fine e poi la Coda

Coda

Tempo di Marcia

5.

Vivace assai

Allegro maestoso

6.

77

p con anima

81

85

f

p

88

f

91

dim.

dolce

Menuetto

Trio

Menuetto da Capo
senza replica, e poi la Coda.

Coda

Fine

K 131

4 Sonatines faciles

Op. 88

Friedrich Kuhlau
(1786–1832)

90

Allegro assai

2.

Andante cantabile

Rondo

Vivace

3. Allegro con affetto

K 131

Allegro burlesco

Allegro molto

4.

Andante con moto

Rondo alla Polacca

4 Sonatines

Le Bouquetier

Op. 151

Anton Diabelli
(1781–1858)

Scherzo

Allegro

Rondo

Allegretto

2. Moderato

Andante religioso

Rondo

Allegro

Allegro moderato

3.

Rondo

Allegretto

Allegro moderato

4.

Largo maestoso

Rondo

Allegro, ma non troppo

134

7 Sonatinen

Musikalische Morgenstunden einer Woche

Op.168

Anton Diabelli
(1781–1858)

Moderato cantabile

Andante cantabile

K 131

Rondo

Allegretto

Allegro moderato

2.

Rondo

Allegretto

Allegro moderato

Andantino

Rondo
Allegro

Allegro moderato

4.

152

Andantino

Rondo

Allegro

156

Tempo di Marcia

5.

158

Marcia funebre

Andante maestoso

Rondo militare

Allegro

Allegro moderato

Andante cantabile

Rondo

Allegro

Allegro moderato

Andante cantabile

Rondo

Allegretto